AF257034

Outhouse Stories

of the

Bradshaw Mts.

By Barb Myers

Native Arizonian – Desert Rat

ISBN - Paperback: 978-1-64873-501-1

Copyright © 2024 Barb Myers

All rights reserved. No part of this book may be used or reproduced in any form whatsoever without written permission, except in the case of brief quotations in critical articles or reviews.

Published By Writers Publishing House
writerspublishinghouse.com

Printed in the United States of America.

My life in Crown King area with an Outhouse
collection inspired me to write about people and
places in the Bradshaw Mtns.

Contents

Chapter One:
Lobe The Wolf
2-13-2014

By David Martin

In the 1960s, while living in the Crown King area, some people found a wolf den, a mother and some cubs. They called Game & Fish in to get rid of the wolves.

They went up to the den and shot into the hole. They asked me to go inside, so I did. There was one wolf pup hiding behind the mother that did not get hit. Lobo. He was raised at the same Hanford folks' place at Fort Misery when the big snow of 1967 forced evacuation of the people. The wolf was left behind. Dave adopted the wolf, or the wolf accepted and adopted Dave.

Tony Nelson, Ron Lips and myself walked into Fort Misery to check on the Hanford's. Helicopter had evacuated them out. Lobo the wolf was left behind and followed Tony Nelson home.

Fang is buried in Crown King. He was a coyote and German Shepard. When we were staying at the Crown King work station ending up the forest job, Fang went poop in Ron Lip's boot right in the square during the big snow of 1967. It was too cold to go outside in the snow.

While in the Spring of 1967, the snow was pretty melted off. We were working in Horsethief. Lobo followed me and loaded up into the old power wagon. I was headed down to Phoenix to see a friend, Jimmy Moon. Lobo adopted me. Lobe taught Fang to jump the six-foot fence and swim in the neighbor's pool.

Lobo was a Mexican wolf. I adopted a female Siberian Husky, "Star." I got her for Lobo. They had two litters together. I have a cupboard full of ashes from the wolves.

After the F.S., I trained wolves for movies. I met a man who lived up in Jackson Hole, O. Benus, who wanted to buy one of my wolves. He liked "Newmac." He was 7/8 wolf. They were in the movie "Mountain Men" by Columbia Pictures. They asked if he knew anyone that has wolves. They called me on Thursday and said to be in Jackson Hole on Saturday.

At the time, I had eleven wolves. All of my wolves did different things, like chase a horse or something. We had no idea what the movie director wanted.

They wanted some growling and snarling, so I had two bitch dogs that hate each other. So, we held the two dogs by their tails while they filmed the dogs. The production cost was $100 per day for the movie shooting. All the wolves were painted green for the buffalo scene.

No one got bit, but one person bent over to throw some food to the "Red Witch" wolf. And the dog was worked up. "Skeana" to corner in Spanish was the head bitch. Charles Heston threw a fake rock at her. She took off and didn't understand why her friend was throwing things at her. I made $45,000 for the scene and was kept on the payroll for some time after that.

"Never Cry Wolf" was another movie. I was a breeder and exhibitor licensed with Federal Agriculture Number 86 CL. My dogs all had ear tags with my license number.

"Journey of Natty Jane." The dog Jed was a wolf dog. This was a Hollywood movie, and he did not like loud noises. I had a dog that was a dead ringer for Jed. So, my dog was a stand-in or stunt dog. He was trained to run along and jump into a moving train car. I got $25,000 for that scene. My dog was also in "The Thing" and "The Artic."

I worked with the wolves in movies for eight or nine years. I got my hip crushed 2-6-1990 doing Father Dowling's mysteries and new Perry Mason series in Colorado. I was doing wardrobe and fell off the back of the forty-foot semi, and that ended my movie days. You cannot have a CDL License and have a plastic body part.

I was called to do the "Dances of the Wolves", but had to turn that down for now. I am in the hospital. Raymond Burr got to meet my daughter. Elizabeth was about six weeks old.

The black Grace Jones woman from New York was doing a musical to make money for Hopi Indian alcoholics. My wife Suzanne and her friend took four wolves to New York to be in the musical.

I live in Crown King, 1906 past Cadillac group, Tarter Claim on Towers Mountain Road. My best friend Gene Doris built a house on the property and has lived there for twenty-five years. The first fifteen years. I had no electricity. That was the one-year APS locked up out in the middle of the night. I was

16 years old when I bought the property in 1972, so I have had the place for 57 years.

Chapter Two:
A Land of Sunshine & Silver

By Barb Myers

During 1871-1872, the Tiger Company extracted 700 tons of ore and shipped fourteen of the richest (worth $10,374) to San Francisco. Arizona bonanza — boot values advanced to

$50 and $100. In a froth of excitement, Editor Marion rejoiced in verse: Ring out wild bells to the wild sky. We've struck it rich and feet are high!

Over-enthusiasm ripened investors for speculation. Throughout February and March, merchants and businessmen in nearby settlements purchased portions of the Tiger Lode. There was no natural route to the Tiger Mine, but soon after its discovery, scheduled pack trains with provisions were winding their way from Wickenburg and Prescott towards the camp. In the hills, twenty miles south of the Tiger Mine, however, roving Indians killed Jacob Snively.

In Central Arizona, the years between 1871 and 1876, despite the exodus of the early 70s, were a period of discovery. Each winter, spring, summer and fall, bands of prospectors left Prescott like ants, leaving their ant hill in search of sweet discoveries.

Grubstake by merchants, professional men and mine speculators were eager for a share of a strike. These prospectors, after a month or so in the hills, entered Prescott bearing carefully-selected mineral samples from their new claims. "Generally speaking, nearly every prospective expedition... finds new mines," comments the U. S. Mining Commissioner in his report for 1873.

Canadian Ed Peck, was lucky. He prospected further and at a nearby spring and found a rich silver float. He knew what to do. Peck lode tested samples whose value ranged from $3,000 to $22,000 per ton. On June 16, 1875, the men quickly staked out 1500 feet along the new bonanza.

On July 2, the Arizona miner created a sensation with an ecstatic article entitled "The Latest, Bigger and Richest." Parties flocked to the Peck Mining District and located extensions, the most attractive being the Silver Prince and the Black Warrior, while Peck and Alexander removed the rich yellow chlorides and black carbonates of silver. Admiring observers called the Peck "truly one of the great mines of the world."

Chapter Three:
Cleator, Az

By Jim Shipman

The namesake of Cleator, AZ is James Patrick Cleator. Mr. Cleator was called Jim or Jimmy or JP, but NEVER just Cleator. JP was born on the Isle of Man, an island in the Irish Sea, July 12, 1870. JP left at age 14 as a cabin boy on the tall sailing ships. One of the interesting stories he used to tell was that on one voyage when they left Liverpool, the docks had gas lanterns, and when they returned, there were electric lights. He sailed around Cape Horn at least twice in his career as a sailor.

JP hit North America in Halifax, Canada. He worked and prospected across Canada down into California and even old Mexico, eventually settling in Arizona. He said he made a lot of money prospecting – more than ever since settling in the area now known as Cleator. He often recalled shaking President Harrison's hand in the Palace Hotel in San Francisco in 1888. He became a naturalized citizen in Redding, CA in 1898.

What is now known as Cleator was born in 1904. The town's original owner was L.P. Nellis, and he christened it Turkey or Turkey Creek, taking its name from mining claims within the town – Turkey and Turkey Gobbler. JP arrived in the Cleator area in 1905 and bought an interest in Nellis' business. The store in Cleator sold many items, and it was also a polling place for area voting. Nellis and Cleator had a recipe for root beer that made mouths water. The business of Nellis and Cleator prospered, and the two went into cattle ranching too. Later, Nellis retired in 1919 and the partners swapped out, keeping the cattle business and Cleator the town. When the area needed a Post Office, the name of the town needed changing, as there was already a community named Turkey with a Post Office. So, JP requested it be named Cleator. The government granted the request in May 1925, and the railroad did likewise in November 1926. The rail retreated from Crown King to Middleton in 1926 and Cleator in 1932. After the rails were removed, Cleator lost much of its area importance.

JP used to say he was raised on the water and stranded in the desert. It is believed that one of the many reasons for JP's much success in life was his story-telling ability, which he was a master at. Without TV or much radio, this was a valuable asset in those days, and he could absolutely mesmerize anyone with his tall tales of sailing ships and prospecting stories. From lanterns to electricity to jet airplanes when he passed on in 1955! This world traveling also explains why JP was 48 before he got married.

Meeting His Wife: Willmetta Pearl Hunt (Pearl) had a sister named Frank (yes, Frank) Baker. Aunt Frank, as she was known, husband owned the Thunderbolt Mine near Cleator down on Turkey Creek. Frank was a friend of JP's. Pearl had another sister, Grace, whose husband also worked in the mining business and owned the Richenbar Mine near Cleator under Black Mesa. It was through these acquaintances and visits to her sisters that she met JP – she lived in Joplin, MO.

On one of Pearl's visits, JP asked her to stay and marry him. But Pearl's mother, Lizzie Cost Hunt, was still alive in Joplin, so she returned to be with her mother. When Pearl's mother passed away, she returned to Cleator and married JP on February 26, 1919.

Friends of JP's kidded him that he had met his "Waterloo" in meeting Pearl. By the way, Pearl ALWAYS CALLED JP "Mr. Cleator" in front of others. Pearl was a very formal and disciplined lady. He had never been married. Pearl, who also had never been married, was born in Joplin, MO. January 7, 1879. Not only was JP already 48, but Pearl was 40 when they tied the knot! Three pregnancies were to follow.

Approximately 1921, Pearl lost her first child, a son, practically at birth – only a few weeks old. In 1923, she was pregnant again, and this time, she didn't want to take any second chances with the medical amenities in Arizona of that time. Plus, she was 44 years young! So, she literally stepped out her front door in Cleator and boarded the train that went through the center of the town and went to Joplin, MO, to successfully bear Elizabeth Ether Cleator (Betty). As soon as Betty and Mother could travel, JP went to Joplin and brought them home to Cleator. They stepped off the train in Cleator and were home. This exact same process was successfully repeated in 1925 with the birth of Thomas Rice Cleator. Also, an interesting side note is that in 1923 for his first daughter's birth, JP

Cleator was 52! And for his last son's birth, he was 55 (and Pearl, even more significantly, was 46).

The Cleator school needed more students, so Betty started first grade at the age of 3. She was able to keep up, so this worked well for both sides. She started at the "old" school near where the Rock schoolhouse now stands. The WPA built the Rock schoolhouse in 1932 during the Great Depression. Her first teacher was Miss Adams, with Mrs. Golthwaite and Mrs. Keller to follow.

Betty's last two years of school, her Junior and Senior years, were in Prescott. She started in the fall of 1936, spending the week and boarding in Prescott, and her dad, JP, would go to get her to return to Cleator for the weekends. She graduated in the spring of 1938 at the age of 15.

Tom followed a similar path, except three years later, and his interests were not as academic as his big sister's – he ran more to cars and mining. After graduating from Prescott High, Tom was drafted at age 18 into the Army Air Corp (later USAF) as a mechanic.

Betty entered the University of Arizona in the fall of 1938. She returned to Cleator for the summers. She graduated with honors from U of A, in the Spring of 1942 at age 19.

Betty taught school in Hayden, AZ, during the school year 1942-43. She was hired to teach the Mexican section (all miner's kids) because of her knowledge of Spanish.

Needing a summer job in 1943, Betty stayed with family friends, the Kinnon family in Phoenix. Mr. Kinnon owned a mine near Cleator and worked it on weekends. The Adams Hotel was a gathering place for out-of-towners and locals in the mining business. The Kinnons visited people at the Adams, and while there with the Kinnons, Betty noticed the American Airlines office. She applied for a job and was immediately interviewed by Mr. James Robb (father of VA Governor Robb). She was hired on the spot as a Reservations and Ticketing person. Mr. Robb later told her he had hired her because he could not throw her off balance, and the kicker was her answer to the question. "Where did you get those beautiful brown eyes?" Betty's response was "God gave them to me! He said he knew he would hire her right then.

Given just enough time to return to Cleator to gather her clothes, she returned to Phoenix and rented a room from friends of the Cleators and started her job with American Airlines. As she was too young (requirement was age 21), she applied for that job as soon as she was of age. She did not even have to interview and got the stewardess job at age 21 in the Spring of 1944.

Chapter Four:
The Golden Triangle

By Barb Myers

Land of extremes. Land of contrasts. Land of surprises. Land of contradictions. Land of such a diversity of origins, motives and ideas that generations must pass before they can ever fully understand each other.

That is Arizona.

The Apache Indians seem to have always been at war with the rest of the human race. They claimed and roamed over an immense territory.

In the midst of this country lies the "great golden triangle." The country inside of this triangle was always regarded as the stronghold of the Apaches, whose boast was that white men never escaped who once got into this. Central Arizona is located within the forbidden limits.

The golden triangle was also known by the miners as the area, from Black Canyon City to Cordes to Prescott to Black Canyon City, rich in gold nuggets and greatly mined area.

"Mexican Joe," who lived in Bumble Bee, paid his APS electric bill with gold nuggets. Ann Tefft told me, "Mexican Joe had a real eye for spotting nuggets. He would just be walking along the road, stop, reach down and pick up a piece of gold. In all my life, I've never found any. How on earth did he?

Chapter Five:

The Crown King School

By Barb Myers

Jon Messenger, far left, entertained the grade school and community of Crown King. Messenger, who is an artist, taught the history of the American cowboy life. Pictured from left to right are: Messenger, Ian Castelanho, Bridgett Ann Mauer, Liberty McNeece, Amanda Myers, Johnathan Ricardo, Elizabeth Martin, Justice McNeece and Richard Brown.

The Crown King School was originally held in an old boarding house, which was remembered by students as "very cold" in 1894-95.

When the railroad came, a one-room schoolhouse was built, and it opened on February 1. 1917.

The money was furnished by the Santa Fe Railroad, Nelson Mining Company and the Bradshaw Reduction Company.

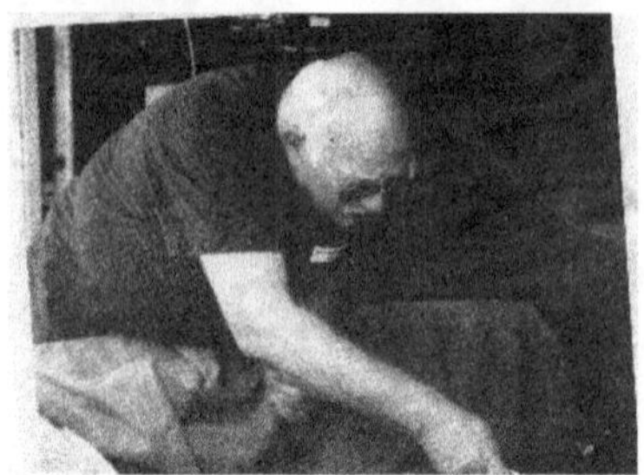

Several; years ago. The school became a two-room operation and boasts a library and computer equipment. There are generally 12-13 students from kindergarten through eighth grade.

The Crown King School

The Crown King School was originally held in an old boarding house which was remembered by students as being "very cold" in 1894 - 95.

When the railroad came, a one-room schoolhouse was built and it opened on February 1, 1917.

The money was furnished by the Santa Fe Railroad, Nelson mining Company and the Bradshaw Reduction Company.

Several years ago, the school became a two-room operation and boasts a library and computer equipment. There are generally 12-13 students from kindergarten through eighth grade.

LIST OF SCHOOL TEACHERS FROM 1894 - 1957

1894 - 1895	Essie B. Nelson - *taught in the boarding house*
1903	Virgie Hite - *she married the sheriff and arrived from Prescott on horseback*
1915 - 1916	Edna Shoe (Layton) *taught in the boarding house*
1916	Helen Harrington Sweet - *George Harrington's daughter*
1918 - 1920	Cora E. Phillips
1920 - 1924	R. S. Patterson
1924 - 1925	Dorch Morgan Wingert
1925 - 1926	Edith Light
1926 - 1928	Edith Keller
1928 - 1930	Miss Beatrice Ready
1930 - 1933	Edith Keller
1933 - 1934	Helen Harrington Sweet
1934 - 1936	Nellie Goldthwaite
1936 - 1937	Mrs. Mildred Beuthel
1937 - 1938	Mr. Floyd S. Kitchen
1938 - 1939	Violet M. Bemis
1939 - 1940	Edith Keller
1940 - 1941	Miss Edna V. Cordes
1941 - 1942	Bernice Moore
1942 - 1943	Ruth Falconer
1943 - 1946	Maria H. Helm
1946 - 1947	Nora Y. Sturm
1947 - 1948	Alice Aly
1948 - 1949	Miss Pauline Sanholdt
1949 - 1950	Naomi Garber
1951 - 1953	Alma Beaty
1953 - 1954	Geneva H. Moores
1954 - 1957	Edith Keller

Chapter Six:
Sw Fore Firefighters

By Barb Myers

Karen Coey thought it was a pretty good idea when Chief Steve Lombardo offered to pay room and board for a week at Bullhead City for learning how to be a clown. "I didn't know what I was getting in for," she says, admitting

L-R. Karen Coey "Electra", Sandy Wells "Sunshine, and Kate Bennett "Smoke" listen to the Fireman (Crash Leyland) and teach fire safety to Crown King Elementary students.

she was too tired to go out and play after the intensive seminar sessions.

In the 1980s, the Colorado Springs Fire Department began to teach young children about fire safety using humor and funny characters. Realizing the retention rate was much higher, police departments across the country adopted the same technique. Each year, a one-week training seminar is offered, sharing these ideas among 15 new students.

Karen Coey and Sandy Wells attended the seminar this year and came back with a program they are now sharing with local schools and police departments.

It isn't all just clowning around. They had to learn educating skills, as well as acting skills. Performing in front of their fellow students was the most difficult part, Karen believes.

Back in Crown King, Karen and Sandy were joined by Crash Layland and Kate Bennett, and their first performance was at Crown King School. They taught the children how to plan an exit drill in their house in case of a fire. They also showed them what a firefighter in smoke protection gear would look like if he came after them in an emergency.

One week later, Coey and Sandy returned to the school and tested the kids for retention. It was 100%

If you missed the show at Crown King, you can watch this dynamic act at Canon School on April 22.

Chapter Seven:
Railroad Days

By Cliff Collup

Towers Mtn. Cabin

The Crown King Mine was the main reason they built the railroad. Frank Murphy was a real gambler. He was told it was impossible to build the Bradshaw Mountain Railroad from Prescott to Crown King. Frank Murphy was a brother of L. G. Murphy, the man Billie the Kid shot. Frank Murphy, his younger brother, sold his cattle ranch in Nebraska and used the money to build the railroad. The infamous cowboy gang, the Dolans that rode against Wyatt Earp, were also involved. The Dolans were half-partners in a cattle ranch with L. G. Murphy. A lot of the money used to build the railroad was blood money. Money also was raised by selling bad stocks.

The DeSoto Mine was a copper mine that the railroad serviced at Middleton. The Germans built the tramway there. Because of its design, it required no engines. It ran on centrifugal (gravity) force.

In 1909, the Pacific Copper Company found a copper vein 150 ft. wide and a shaft over 400 feet deep at Silver Creek. (I had all the assays on the patented land.) The P.C.C. had a 40-foot right of way from Silver Creek to build a road on. Believe it or not, they used Keystone Packard trucks with hard wheels, chain driven, and hauled 15 tons per load from Silver Creek to Crown King. The report on the copper shipment at Humboldt was 21% copper, 200 ounces silver,.05 ounces gold per ton. Stocks were sold on the New York Stock Exchange at $1 per share, and one million shares were sold.

The Pacific Copper Company was also a big user of the railroad. They had seven cars of champagne and five cars of distillate oil shipped to Crown King. They had approximately 500 men working at the Silver Creek Mine, and it was the first all-electric mine in the Bradshaws. They used the oil distillate that powered a D.C. voltage generator that supplied electricity to open-wound motors and light bulbs.

When a railroad is built, the government allows a 10-acre easement on both sides of the track, and you pay so much per foot per altitude. In shipping ore out of a place, the railroad charges a percentage of the value of the ore. So, if you ship pure gold, you pay the percentage!

In 1929, the smelter in Mayer blew up, so the mines in Crown King were going to have to transfer the ore to Douglas. The mines shut down during the war when they needed it the most.

The last run to Crown King in 1934 by the Bradshaw Mountain Railroad was to deliver a baby buggy to a Forest Service Ranger named H. J Tuney. The CCC Boys (Civilian Conservation Corps) had already built his house out of rocks. It even had a basement. The house still stands today in Crown King.

Chapter Eight:
Deer Hunting

Told by Cliff Collup

Cliff Collup - Log Cabin Built 1864

During the depression about 1932, we lived on beans and venison. We were out of 30-30 shells, but we had some 22 shells. Up in the meadow stood a great big 5-point buck, only about 100 yards from the house.

My Uncle Hays was a very good shot. He took aim at the buck and hit it right between the eyes. Bang! went the 22 rifle and down went the buck!

Uncle Hays ran up, lifted up the deer's foreleg, and stabbed the jugular vein to start bleeding it.

The deer jumped between Hays' legs went off across the meadow with Hays astraddle, hanging on his horns.

The deer jumped the fence at the south end of the meadow and with Hays still on his back, they went over the hill and down through the brush towards Ash Basin. After about ten minutes of this, the deer had lost enough blood and died. Hays walked back to the cabin, shirt torn off, pants ragged, shoes off, and scratched from head to toe. All he had to say was, "The son-of-a-gun didn't get away from me!"

So, we all went down and brought the deer back. That night we had liver and onions for supper and Uncle Hays started making jerky. That's what the Collups lived on, venison jerky, beans and sourdough biscuits.

What we found when we butchered that back out was that the 22 shells had hit the eye guard, so it hadn't killed him, just stunned him.

Chapter Nine:
Sheep at Cordes... Baaa

By Barb Myers

Mantarola Sheep Company trucks 4,000 sheep from Mohave, California, to Cordes, then trails them in two bands from Beaverhead-Grief Hill to Williams. "Trailing is good for the ewes," says Joe Mantarola, "because it keeps their weight down, conditions them for breeding, and accustomed them to higher altitudes in slow stages."

One herder is responsible for the sheep. One camper is in charge of the six burros, cooking and moving camp. Water is carried in five-gallon wooden kegs because they can't camp on the water holes. The sheep travel three to five miles per day. The trip

takes about 25 days and is 100 miles on foot. Some sheep have bells, so the herder can hear them at night if something happens. Coyotes are a menace to the sheep, as one to two sheep are taken down every night.

Cordes was greatly involved in the construction of the Verde River Sheep Bridge or "Sheep Crossing."

Built in 1940-41 by Frank Auza to provide safe passage for large herds of sheep. It is a link between their winter and summer ranges.

The suspension cable bridge was the last remaining structure of its type in the Southwest. The "Man that got the cable" was Henry Cordes, since he was knowledgeable about the Blue Bell Copper Mine near Mayer. Cordes helped Auza and two Mexicans gather two 900-foot, 1-3/4" lengths of cable from an abandoned overhead tramway. Cordes also obtained the bridge's guy wires from the Golden Turkey Mine. The mine owners gave the cables to the sheepmen.

When asked how he got involved with the bridge, Cordes said, "I'm involved with everything the sheepherders ever did. My father was too! They brought me their problems, and I tried to help them the best I could."

Chapter Ten:

*Looking Back At Crown
Kings Towers Maintain*

By Barb Myers

Most people think Towers' Mountain is named because of the myriad towers on the top of the mountain. Actually, the mountain was named after George W. Tower, the first prospector to patent a mining claim in the Pine Grove Mining District.

In 1871, Towers originally surveyed and applied for the (Green Mountain Mining Claim) at Prescott. Arizona was still a territory. In 1881, ten years later, his claim was founded and patented. Mr. Tower was also the first prospector in the Southern Bradshaw's to melt his gold into bars. Gold molds were found with the "pine tree" emblem, meaning Pine Grove Mining District.

Mr. Tower was a well-educated mining engineer and superintendent of the Tiger Mine. Mr. Tower also traded with the Apache Indians. A horse trail passed over Towers' Mountain, passing Indians never bothered the prospector as long as they received a horse or a gift of food. Tower was friendly, but never personal with the Apache's.

Glenn and Elsie VanTilborg acquired the property on back taxes after George W. Tower's death. Story goes that one of the VanTilborg boys, Don and Grant, were drinking and caught the house on fire.

The property was then sold to the Collup Family (F.D. Collup & W.D. Collup), which has remained for three generations to the Collups.

Uncle Buck's Cleator Cowboy Chili

By Paul Welch

Makes 2 crockpots full

- 3 yellow onions (chopped)
- 3 lbs meat (Elk or Beef best) – brown in bacon grease
- 1 lrg can Diced Tomatoes
- 2 sm cans Diced Green Chilies
- 1 or 2 sm cans Diced Jalapenos
- 1 lrg can of Elpato Mexican Tomato Sauce
- 1 lrg can of Red Chilies – Diced
- ½ Pound Bacon – chopped - brown lightly (in beans only)
- 1 lb pinto beans – cook separately
- 1 Tbl spoon of Coriander
- 1 Tbl spoon of Cumin
- 1 Bay Leaf – put in beans
- 6 cloves of Garlic – chopped finely
- Salt & Pepper to taste
- 4 heaping Tbls Chili Powder
- ½ Cup Pepper – yellow can with red peppers
- Cook beans and meat separately.
- Cook beans 24 hours until soft.

Famous Outhouses

In the Bradshaw Mtns.

New Publin Outhouse - Between Store & Fire Station

34

Cookie Jar Outhouse

Phil Beverly Ranch - Campe Verde

Meat Smoker Hotel Salon Old Crown King Hotel

Heater at Hotel Salon Old Crown King Hotel

Cleator Outhouse

Old Fire Station Outhouse

Cleator

Water Bobus

Pretty Little Well House

42

Sinclaus Green House the Mill

Chapter Eleven:

Happenings On the Crown King Road;
Grapevine Washout of '72

David Rhodes and Family

"Don't let this dry-looking country fool ya. It can rain around here!" says Walt Diskin of Mayer.

In the summer of 1972, the skies opened up and dropped approximately 10 inches of water in 30 minutes. It wiped enormous boulders off the mountainside, causing a severe washout of the Crown King Road. There were so many boulders that came down the hill, they just scattered, crushing all the oak trees and vegetation; a strong oak aroma filled the air.

The road was closed for two weeks while the road was being rebuilt by two large dozers to make it passable for the mail trucks to get through. During the rebuilding Crown King Forest Service Ranger, Ray Adare hiked through the washed-out area to the bottom, meeting the mail truck from Mayer, swapping mail bags, then hiked back up to Crown King.

Walt Diskin was the road grader for over 18 years, driving the D-6 Cat pull blade grader. Walt maintained all the local roads. But there was a lot of traffic. I remember killing a lot of black timber rattlers in the Swastika Hills area, and I saw many deer.

Walt Diskin D-6 Cat 1972

Walt was born in Humboldt and has lived in Mayer since 1936.

David Rhodes heads into the Cleator Bar in May. A variety of visitors stop by, some on their way to Crown King. PHOTOS BY DAVID WALLACE/THE REPU

Cleator 2013

David Rhodes savors his cherished bar. "I remember moving here and there was no lights to the north, and you could see the Milky Way, even on a full-moon night," Rhodes said about Cleator.

David Rhodes Saving his Bar

David Rhodes abandoned the city
for the solitude of the Arizona desert.
There, in the ghost town of Cleator, he found
a life much fuller than he had expected.

Chapter Twelve:
Bear Attacks It's Reflection

By Barb Myers

Outside of Cleator, Az., is an old mine, which was mostly mined for silver, patented in 1876.

One cool morning, a bear came nosing about and saw himself in the beautiful glass door.

The bear attacked itself, of course.

The man living in the mine (name withheld) says, "That was enough for him and decided then to build a cabin."

The prospector lived for the winter in the mine, which was equipped with a wood stove, even though the mine stayed at a constant 72 degrees.

The prospector's friend, Kelly, helped him build all the beautiful rock work sealing off the entrance, and also on the inside, the native stone dried in the home.

But what happened to the bear? Who knows! Maybe he's still out there looking for himself.

Chapter Thirteen
South Bradshaw Mountain 1970 Roundup

By Annette Pock

In September 1970, my husband, Marty, was discharged from the United States Navy. It was at the end of the Vietnam War. When he was discharged, Marty, myself, and our 2-month-old daughter, Billie Jolene, went to his parents' home. His parents, Don and Rosemary Pock, lived at the

Annette Pock

headquarters of the NO Ranch located along the Agua Fria River on the south end of the Bradshaw Mountains in Arizona.

Fall roundup was about to begin, so we decided to work through the fall roundup on the ranch. It had a chuck wagon style cupboard that folded down, providing a counter. We got to sleep in this cabin, since we had a small baby. Everyone else

50

slept in the barn up the hill in a little tin shed next to the cabin or wherever they could find a place to throw their bedroll.

There were a lot of blackberries all along the creek from the windmill down. They were so plentiful that they were a nuisance to cowboys riding horseback. I imagine that between the droughts and the fires, the blackberries have disappeared. Are they hardy enough to survive and return with a little rain?

While at Packer, it was Halloween. I carved out a pumpkin and wanted to dry the seeds. I laid the seeds outside to dry on a board. In the morning, the seeds had disappeared. The mice had packed them off. No pumpkin seeds for us, but the mice were ready for winter.

Vernon Martin was a cowboy who worked in the Bradshaw Mountains a lot, including the NO Ranch. Vernon and another hand were in the process of cleaning the barn that was located up the hill and north of the cabin. Amongst the hay was found about a case of dynamite. The box was decomposed, and only the sticks were left. They were CAREFULLY cleaned, removing the dynamite. It was left from old mining days.

Roundup took in the Milk Ranch, Shamrock Mountain and Bird Springs. It took about 2 weeks to work the area, all on horseback. Camp was moved south to Tip Top. Cattle that were to be sold and shipped were also down the mountain to Tip Top also.

Tip Top could be called a cow camp, where a full-time cowboy lived most of the time. The house and facilities there were originally well built, consisting of three rooms: kitchen, living/dining room and bedroom. A bathroom was added later on one end of the screened-in porch. There was a cistern outside the kitchen with water piped in. On the kitchen end of the porch was a pantry/cupboard stocked year around with canned foods in case a traveler was going by and needed to eat, especially when traveling was done by horseback or foot. A drifting prospector stopped by occasionally, leaving the place clean and picked up.

I remember washing cloth diapers in the sink when I was there. At the time, it seemed less work than the 2-hour bumpy, rough trip down to the NO Ranch headquarters, where there was a washing machine. No cowboys offered their help for that job!

During the 1870s, Tip Top was an active silver/gold mine. The history of Tip Top is an account worth reading in itself.

Roundup from Tip Top included Humbug, Carpenter Canyon, Cottonwood Canyon and Houston Springs. These places were active and inhabited by people during the mining days. There was a place called the Racetrack, so-called because it was the only flat spot on the ranch.

After about a month of gathering and branding cattle to be sold and shipped, including those from the Packer area, the cowboys drove them on horseback to the No Ranch headquarters. From the headquarters, they were loaded and transported by modern cattle hauling trucks to their next destination.

That was a good memory in our young married life. But roundup was over, and just like the cattle, we moved on in life to other jobs, homes and children.

It is now 2021, 51 years past, but it doesn't seem so long ago.

Chapter Fourteen
The Abby House

By Loraine Elliott

Abby House - Had a Fly Catcher

In 1965, Mr. Abbey and I would go to the General Store and fight over the over-ripe bananas. One day he invited me up to sit in his rocking chair. I went up to his house and saw that he had made a sturdy rocking chair. The seat of the chair was made out of a big flat rock; thus, it really was a rocking chair!

Mr. Abbey moved all the immense rocks around the swimming pools by himself. The swimming pools actually held tanks for the irrigated gardens. He grew the most beautiful, largest dahlias I have ever seen. They were plate size. Huge tomatoes and vegetables of every sort were grown and given to his Crown King acquaintances.

I was always flattered that Mr. Abbey addressed me as his friend, because he was a most unusual and delightful man. Mr. Abbey appeared to weigh more than one hundred pounds. People would comment to him that he couldn't have moved those huge rocks by himself. He would reply, "You can move anything if you know the art of leverage!"

Chapter Fifteen
Rabid Bobcat At Tip Top

By Don Pock

I'm an old retired cowboy living in the Willcox country now, but I spent most of my cowboying days in the New River and Southern end of the Bradshaw Mountains. I ran the old N-O Ranch for 10 years (they renamed it to Boulder Creek Ranch).

I think most of you people know old Vernon Martin. He was raised and lived around Bumble Bee and Crown King all his life. Well, I would hire Vernon when I needed an extra cowboy. He was a good hand.

I had Vernon staying at the Tip Top Camp. He was by himself, so I would go up and check on him pretty often and take him a few groceries. I lived at the headquarters on the Agua Fria River.

Well, one morning I got up, loaded my dogs, and took off up there. It was about 10 miles through rugged country.

When I arrived there and went by the barn, the horses were fed, so I knew he must still be alive. I pulled on over to the house, and there was Vernon, in the yard, messing with some sort of varmint.

I wondered what the heck he was doing. Well, he was gutting a bobcat, and I asked him what happened. I helped him gut it, and we put it in my truck, then went inside to have coffee. He started telling his story about the cat.

Vernon went to the barn to feed the horses. When he got there, he heard a growling noise. He opened the barn door, and there on the hay was this cat. He said the cat was looking at him, growling and slobbering, and Vernon thought he must be rabid. Well, he had his gun in his chaps in the saddle room. So, he closed the barn door and went and got it. He came back, opened the door, and the cat was still sitting there. He drew a bead on him and shot. The cat jumped out a window and into the barnyard.

Vernon closed the door and ran around there, and the cat charged him. He tried to shoot again, but that was his last shell. He said he threw the gun at the cat, but he kept coming. So Vernon grabbed his hat and whipped the cat in the face while he retreated.

Finally, the cat ran off into a little draw. Vernon said he grabbed his gun and ran to the house to get more shells. There was a screened porch around the side of the house. When Vernon came out, the cat was right there. When the cat saw him, he jumped and hit the screen and hung there. Vernon shot him.

I could see where his claws were hanging in the screen. Anyway, after Vernon killed the cat, I took him to the Fish and Game, and he was rabid! Everyone thought we should take the rabies shots, because we always have cuts on our hands. So, we went every morning at 4 a.m. to Phoenix and got shots. We had one in the belly every day for 14 days. The shots didn't hurt me much. I'm kinda fat. But Vernon was slim, and he would say "oouch!"

I miss the old times–but not the shots!

Chapter Sixteen:

What's Happening In Cleator?

By Barb Myers

Cleator Bar is now open Mon–Fri from 8am to 6 pm and Sundays 10 am to 6 pm. Free coffee too!

Proprietor Dave Rhodes Jr. is from Delaware, Ohio. He came to Cleator in the Spring of 1998, where he lived in his at Poland and Turkey

Creek for four months. Dave lost 110 pounds in 86 days, and since mid-September, he has lost an additional 40 pounds. He moved to the Cleator house in late August, after Dave and his father, David Hanesworth Rhodes, Sr. purchased the liquor license from Caroline Ripley. They received permission to enter the building and open a business.

Grand opening of the newly enlarged bar was celebrated in grand style. Larry and Sue Brethauer helped with the BBQ, bringing food, including home-made bread; Charlie Olachea furnished the ribs, and Dave cooked ribs, turkey and chicken.

Dave lived in Phoenix for 20 years, where he was a bouncer at clubs, and also worked as a bounty hunter in 1989. Dave will celebrate his birthday on February 21st!!

David Rhodes, Jr. Died 2013 at 49

Chapter Seventeen:
Crown King's Chinese Hutches

By Barb Myers

Along Crown King Road in the Crazy Basin area are the Chinese hutches, which were used as shelters. Remains of cement floors used for tent houses are scattered along the old railroad bed.

The earliest Chinese settlers came to Arizona just after it became a territory of the United States in 1863. With the need for transportation and communication with the Northeast came the construction of the railroads. The Chinese were available. They were disciplined laborers, willing to take jobs few others wanted and work for lower wages. Most of these Chinese laborers were section graders, leveling the terrain upon which tracks were laid.

In 1904, the Chinese built the Bradshaw Mountain Railroad, or as it was called locally, "Frank Murphy's Impossible Railroad." Clinging tenaciously to the sides of the lofty Bradshaws, with more kinks than a cheap lariat, the laborers toiled daily until the railroad was built. There were 12 switchbacks with turns so tight that passengers in the caboose could look across and see the engine going the other way.

The railroad was worth every penny of the cost. By 1907, the mines at Tiger, Big Bug, Turkey Creek, Pine Grove and Crown King produced over a million dollars in gold and/*89 silver. By 1920, the days of glory were over when both the Poland and Crown King lines were abandoned.

Chapter Eighteen:
Doll Parachutes Into Crown King

By Cliff Collup

My brother, Willard D. Collup, often stayed with the Glenn and Elsie Van Tilborg family, mostly during the winter, when foot travel was difficult to the top of Towers Mountain where he lived at Spud Ranch.

Willard D. Collup

Willard was fond of Van Tilborg's daughter, Mildred. Willard and Mildred went to grade school together at the Crown King School. Willard later went into the Marine Corps. During this time, Mildred met a man named Vernon Warren. They were married and had a daughter named Verna Warren. Mildred died during childbirth at age 21. The girl, Verna, was raised by her grandparents, Elsie and Glenn Van Tilborg.

In 1945, when Verna was about five or six years old, the pilot who had been fond of her mother flew a D.C.-3 over Crown King and dropped out a doll to the girl.

He came over the top of Towers Mountain through the Del Pasco Saddle, then he did a nose dive roaring towards the Crown King Mine. Just before that pint, he pulled up and flew just over Main Street. As he was flying by, he pushed the doll with her parachute out the window, intending to have it land in the Van Tilborg's yard. Instead, it flew back in the window at him – he pushed it out again, and the third time, it finally went down, landing in Main Street in front of the store.

Everyone in Crown King turned out, as it was the most exciting thing they had ever seen! After he shoved the doll out the window, the pilot pulled up on the stick and up over the California Mountain. The shaking, rattling plane barely made it over the top.

The pilot thought it was a pretty exciting ride too! And the lady, Verna, still has the doll.

Chapter Nineteen:
Tom And I And The Tigers In Cleator

By Barb Myers

When the paramedic stuck the needle into his arm, Tom, but in a semi-conscious state, says, "Those dams Wallapye Tigers."

The paramedic looked around cautiously and asks Carolyn, "What's he talking about tigers?"

When Amanda and I first moved to Cleator, I had never heard of such an insect. But when the weather gets hot in the late spring, these blood sucking bugs come out. The Wallapye Tigers (Chinese Kissing Beetles) look like a small cockroach with wings and have a long snout nose.

They live in the wood and come out at night to feed. The Wallapye Tiger first injects you with an anesthesia to numb the area, then proceeds to suck your blood. You don't feel anything until the next morning. The bug bite area hurts, itches and swells up from the poison.

Living in the little wooden shack, I bug bombed and sprayed the hell out of the wood inside and out. It did slow them down, but we continued to get bitten. The bugs have wings and still get to you. I was going to bail out of the house and sleep in the back of my truck because I was so bitten up.

Tom Dixon and I decided to head over to the

Barb Myers house in Cleator. Notice the "outdoor bath."

Verde River for a few days to get some relief. It was a long, hot, rough six-hour drive. The water in the river sure felt good, jumping into a big deep swimming hole. We did some cat fishing, but they wouldn't bite during the day. We could see these big two-foot catfish in the deep-water hole, but they weren't feeding. It was just too hot! After I got the truck stuck in the soft, hot sand, Tom spent an hour getting the vehicle out. Then we just laid under some trees by the river for the rest of the day. We planned to night fish when the cats would bite, but as the air cooled down, we chose to get some rest and sleep. I was half sick from the 30 Wallapye bug bites on my arms, legs and butt, and adding the hot weather, I was not feeling too great. I enjoyed Tom Dixon's company and protection with his 357 pistol.

The Verde River was beautiful. The Sheep Bridge Crossing was really neat, and I would like to go there again.

When Tom and I returned home to Cleator, Indian Joe was sitting on the porch. He had an interesting article about the Wallapye Tigers in a National Geographic Magazine. The gnarly insects eat rat feces and blood from animals and humans. The Wallapye Tiger also carries a rare disease that humans get. Sometimes the disease doesn't attack for 10 years or more. This disease damages the nervous system and causes respiratory problems.

The good news is, if a certain type of lizard lives in the area, the lizards carry something in them that counteracts the disease from the Wallapye

Tigers. Indian Joe says, "Not to worry, Cleator has this good kind of lizards." What a story. Are these insects native to Arizona? Or did they come in from another country when the miners populated the area? During the higher population time, the Arizona Department of Agriculture shipped some special flies to Cleator from the Macassar Jungle.

They were put in the outhouses and fed on human feces to keep the shitters clean. The locals call the flies "shit bees." When the mines shut down and the people moved out, the flies died. But the dam Wallapye Tigers are still there. So, look out!

I will never forget the day when I was all bit up and miserable. My friend, Tom, brought me over a 30 pack of Bud Light. I ask, "What's that for?" Tom replies, "Medicine." He gave me a smile, then left. **I'll never forget you, Tom Dixon. Barb**

Chapter Twenty:
Alisson Dodge Cleator

By Barb Myers

An old English woman who lived in one of the shacks with no windows and no electricity was enjoying her later years in the Bradshaws. Her house was always messy and cluttered. She didn't have much to live on either, but she always had her proper afternoon tea from England.

One day a man stopped in Cleator. It took a while before she recognized him being her first husband of many years gone past. Alisson was in her twenties, and he being younger than her, about 14 or 15 when they were married. Alisson being a teacher taught her young husband to read and write. But the marriage ended in divorce, and each of them went their separate ways.

When they met again some 50 years later in Cleator, he had since become a successful businessman. He explained to Alisson how he was still in love with her, and also grateful to her teaching him how to read and write. He asked her to come live at his hacienda in Mexico, which was a large three-story house with servants. He would take care of her the rest of her life. But she chose her simple life in the small railroad town of Cleator.

Goes to show money isn't everything. And for most people, happiness can't be bought. Some people can't get away from the mystical Bradshaw Mountains.

Famous Outhouses

In the Bradshaw Mtns.

Towers Mt. Rd

M Gladiator Rd

Peck Mine - Kelly Painter

76

The Pavilion Outhouse

Hite Outhouse

Bloody Basin Rd. (The Hutch)

Swasika Mine Outhouse

Spud Ranch or Green Mtn. Mine

Wagner Mine Outhouse

Eastern Outhouse Samy Wells

Oriental Mine - Peck Canyon

Girls Outhouse

Chapter Twenty-One:
Molly the Donkey

By Barb Myers

Tom Cleator - Molly the Donkey

Near Cleator lived a prospector named St. Lewis. Occasionally, St. Lewis would take his donkey to see Tom Cleator. One afternoon, Lewis, Molly the donkey and Tom Cleator were enjoying some beers. The men filled up a spittoon full of beer for Molly.

A visitor to this area came in and drank a few cold ones with the group. The donkey, that had a little too much beer, leisurely went outside. When she saw the brand new, bright red, shiny Cadillac, she didn't like it at all! So, she proceeded to kick the hell out of the car. A few minutes later, the owner of the red Cadillac decided to head back to Phoenix. He saw what the donkey had done to his brand-new car. He was furious! He stormed back into the bar, yelling, "Your donkey ruined my car and I'm going to sue you!"

Tom Cleator calmly responded, "She isn't our donkey. We don't know who she belongs to. She just wanders in here occasionally from out there somewhere." Well, the man left pretty mad.

Chapter Twenty-Two:
Crown King General Store

By Barb Myers

The general store was built in 1904 by Ely S. Perkins. Instead of money, tokens were at the time when miners cashed their paychecks. They were given tokens to ensure they only spent their money at the store. Ely Perkins had two daughters, Carrie and Marhta, who died of mercury poisoning in 1915.

CROWN KING
GENERAL STORE
Ghost Town Books
Bradshaw Mtn History
Maps - TShirts - Hats
Gifts, plus....
DELICIOUS HOMEMADE
FUDGE
ALL DIFFERENT FLAVORS
Buy One or More Lbs.
and get 1/4 Lb. FREE
WITH THIS AD
Expires 12/31/99

In Crown King
for fine dining it's
THE MILL
Exquisite View - Historic Surroundings
Home Baked Breads - Meats Smoked on Site
(520) 632-7133
Open Friday - Saturday - Sunday

(For those coming early or staying after the Mining History Association Annual Conference in Prescott, June 7-10, 2012, Herb Shepard has sent the following suggestion for a day trip/side trip to the old mining town of Crown King.)

Crown King, a historic gold mining town in the heart of the Bradshaw Mountains mining area, is only 20 miles southeast of Prescott as the crow flies. Driving to Crown King takes about 1 hour and 45 minutes to travel about 65 miles. The hour part of the trip is the last 27 miles, a good dirt road (F.S. 259, Crown King Road) from Interstate 17 to the town. The road follows the old railroad route to the mines and has 4 scenic 180-degree switchbacks.

Crown King is an active mining ghost town that never completely died. There are about 100 full-time residents and 400 summer cabins, mostly owned by people that live in Phoenix. When Phoenix is 110 degrees, Crown King is in the 80s because of its 6,000-foot elevation. In the 1890's, the southern Bradshaws was one of the most active mining areas. Bradshaw City once had 5,000 people before the population migrated to Crown King. The mines and towns are within the Prescott National Forest. The historic mines include the Crown King, War Eagle, Del Pasco, Oro Bella, Tiger, Philadelphia, and Lincoln. Several mines may be back into operation. The Gladiator Mine plans to reopen this year. It was last run in 1986-1988 with about 70 miners, and still has the mill and equipment as it was left at that time.

The story of the railroad to Crown King is nearly as interesting as the mining history. The railroad had reached Prescott in 1893. The potential freight traffic from the mines in the Bradshaws had already attracted attention. In 1901, Frank M. Murphy and his investors incorporated the Bradshaw Mountain Railroad Company. The 28-mile-long line started in Mayer, where it connected with Murphy's Prescott & Eastern. The first 12 miles from Mayer to Turkey Creek descended from 4,400 feet to 3,501 feet in elevation. The last 16 miles climbed to 5,835 feet at Crown King. That steep climb required 9 switchbacks, a 142-foot-long tunnel, and a 393 foot long, 70-foot-high wooden trestle. The line was opened in May 1904 and operated until 1926, when it was abandoned. A second branch line, 8 miles long, was also constructed to Poland in the Big Bug Mining District and started operation in 1902.

Crown King has a small but active historical society and museum. A walking tour of the sites in town has just been put together.

The Chamber's website, crownkingfun.com, has more information. Driving directions will be available at the MHA registration area.

News from Crown King . . .

by Barbara Myers & Bob Helgeson

Friends gathered at The Mill in Crown King to help Lorraine Elliot celebrate her 92nd Birthday. From L-R, Kathleen 'Kip' Casey, Lorraine, Colleen Ormsby, Tim Kenney, all of Crown King, and Linda Colvin, Kip's daughter from Tucson. Forty or more people came for the celebration which was hosted by Mike and Sam Christy of The Mill.

About 350 runners are expected to arrive in Crown King for the end of the 50K & 50 Mile Crown King Run on Saturday, March 20th. The Crown King Saloon will host the meal and ending ceremonies this year.

Dave Rhodes at Cleator Bar says Thank You, Everyone! Stop and see the changes he has made.

Crown King Community Church will hold an Easter Sunrise Service at Vista Point; the regular service will be at 11:00 a.m. There will be an Easter Egg Hunt at The Mill at 12:30 with prizes.

A group of puppeteers from Deer Valley Baptist Church, Junior and Senior High centered on cleaning up the sewage system in Crown King downtown, and property lines and set-backs. Sheriff Buck Buchanan said that a third sargent is to be assigned between the Black Canyon and Mayer Stations. Buchanan also explained that 15-18 year olds are tried in Adult Court, but can't be housed in adult jails. Presently they are being sent to Maricopa County, but Yavapai will have to budget more, as Maricopa as advised they will soon be charging $110 per day per criminal youth housed.

Bruce Michael Wilson, author and friend of Crown King, died of cancer on January 16, 1999. The following is taken from his memorial service, written by his wife, Jan: spent a couple of years as a Prevention Patrolman and was then put in charge of Fire Prevention on the Crown King Ranger District, as well as being in charge of the Horse Thief Basin Recreation area. I eventually became head of the Recreation Staff on the District, but quit the Forest Service when the Crown King District was disbanded in 1979. The huge Castle Creek Fire burned up the east side of the Bradshaws during our last season. We bought a house in Crown King in 1977 which we lived in when we were not living at Towers Mountain. We still own the house and use it as a summer home.

History has always been a

Tranquil Moments

Steal away to some quiet corner
Steal away for just awhile,
It heals the body, soul and spirit
And gives a true and happy smile.

Take a walk and see the beauty -
Mountains high "and breathe the air,"
Thank the Lord for all creation
He allows for us to share.

In the stillness of a corner
Or majestic mountains tall,
He provides us tranquil moments,
Hears the smallest voice and call.

In serenity and beauty
Stillness of the night or day,
Ask believing in God's promise -
Ask believing... steal away.

Katherine Smith Matheney

94

Vernon Martin & Barb Myers

The General Store

The General Store was built in 1904 by Ely S. Perkins. Instead of money, tokens were used at that time when miners cashed their paychecks. They were given tokens to ensure they only spent their money at the store. Ely Perkins had two daughters, Carrie and Martha, who died of mercury poisoning in 1915.

Some tokens used by miners.

Bob Patterson, owner of the General Store, 1924 - 1938.

Robert "Old Man" Patterson, beside the General Store, attempting to dig his car out of the snow, January 8, 1937.

The General Store, as it looks today, with horses out front.

Vernon Martin

Vernon Martin, long-time area resident, started riding burros at age 6 and became a cowboy at age 15.

Vernon and sons Billy, aged 7, and Danny, aged 5, in 1945.

Vernon guarding his
claim at his cabin in
Bradshaw City, 1950.
The cabin was built
in 1945.

Vernon's father, W. J. Martin, at his claim in
Bradshaw City in 1946.

Crown King Y2K Party

Swastika Mine

Bradshaw Mountains
Yavapai County
Arizona

Longitude W 112   Latitude N 34

Friday, December 31, 1999
Saturday, January 1, 2000
Sunday, January 2, 2000

FRIDAY

Begin civil twilight	7:09 a.m.
Sunrise	7:36 a.m.
Sun transit	12:33 p.m.
Sunset	5:29 p.m.
End civil twilight	5:57 p.m.

Moonset	1:16 p.m. on preceding day
Moonrise	2:09 a.m.
Moon transit	8:01 a.m.
Moonset	1:47 p.m.
Moonrise	3:05 a.m. on following day

Phase of the Moon
Waning crescent with 29% of the Moon's visible disk illuminated.

Don't forget the total lunar eclipse at 8:00 p.m., Thursday, January 20, 2000.

Chapter Twenty-Three:

Bringing In Y2K at Swastika Mine (2000)

By Barb Myers

No electricity, no water, only batteries, kerosene, good company and the breath-taking beauty of the Southern Bradshaws over New Year's Day 2000, 8:35 a.m. Surprise; it's morning. The sky is blue. The sun is shining, making the snowflakes glisten as they come drifting down to form white patches on the ground.

Battery-powered radio news reports indicated only computer glitches: one satellite went down for two hours. Some banks were open to show were

101

open to show all was okay. A US Treasury person went to an ATM and withdrew $20.

We listened to a Health Talk show broadcasting from Hawaii. Their tip for the day was, if you have heart burn in the night, sleep on your left side

Virgil, the caretaker, and our host, said he would not kick dogs or women in the new millennium, his New Year's Resolution. His dog, Sabor, kept trying to kiss me because John Calvin and Leo went outside to shoot off about 500 rounds with pistols and also blow up something with dynamite. They were determined to rob me of my

nap time. Margie collected small pieces of granite to etch on them "Swastika, New Year 2000."

On the third day, Sunday, January 2, 2000, at 9:06 a.m., more snow fell: five to six inches at an elevation of 5,000 feet with the temperature in Margie's room at 39 degrees while it was 34 degrees outside. Margie and Virgil stayed up through the night, tending to the fires to keep the house warm.

John and Halem take off from home in his pickup truck but soon after are seen walking back up the hill to the house. The truck's front tire went flat and pulled the truck over towards the edge of the road with only two inches between them and the ravine. The road is now blocked so no one can get in or out. With the

weather report predicting 18 degrees and more snow everyone decided to stay put.

On the fourth day, Monday, January 3, 2000, I drove out to Bloody Basin to pick up my daughter, Amanda, and drive back to the mine over snowy and icy roads. Margie was going to try to make it out in her two-wheel drive but the roads turned to complete ice and that idea was abandoned. The big decision that night was what to eat. Would it be chicken, pheasant or turkey? The turkey goes first along with a pot of beans.

That day Virgil had warned us of ghost reports in the back room of the main house. That night when all the lights were out, only the fireplace glowed. The ghost of the Swastika or Silver Prince showed, leaving his initials (JLJ) sketched on a cup. We all had the he-be-bees after that and no one said a word. We just all looked at each other.

The fifth day, Tuesday, January 4, 2000, we decided to attempt going out on the back road that was built by the Germans. We drive 10 minutes to the fish pond with the narrow road sloping to the sides with deep drop-offs, ruts and boulders. After talking over the situation, Margie and I decide to hike the two-mile road. I could see a rollover happening. It was that rough and dangerous.

Back to the mine. Time to chain up the vehicles. There in the barn I found an old pair of bailing wire modified chains. With our limited tools, Margie and I unmodified the chains to fit her truck. Once again, we said our good-byes to Virgil and started down the ice-slicked road. Margie had stopped and I walked back to her to answer her question. "How was it?" I tells him it was slippery, even with a four-wheel drive-in tow and with chains. Taking time to discuss the situation, we decided to abandon Margie's vehicle and come back for it when the ice thaws. She rode out with me, one mile in 30 minutes. When we finally reached the Crown King Road, Margie cries out in glee, "Freedom at last!"

Chapter Twenty-Four:
*Cleator's New Rock School House:
circa 1931*

By Barb Myers

The "new" rock school house was built in 1931 by the Civil Conservation Core (CCC boys through the (WPS) Works Progress Administration. James P. Cleator, Jon Cordes and some other men installed beautiful solid fir wood floors because the cement floor was too cold. As of today, none of

the wood has warped. The men also worked for two days to bust a hole through the two-foot thick cement walls to run electric wiring inside.

The school house hosted many big dances, with records played by a hand cranked phonograph or Vernon and Joe Martin would come from Bumble Bee and play guitars. George and Lawton Champe (world champion bronc buster) would ride to Cleator from Castle Hot Springs along with other cowboys.

Folks would come from every direction to dance all-night, then ride home the next day. Betty Cleator says, "I remember ordering lots of hot dogs and buns for Halloween and everyone came from miles around. We saved big Quaker Oats boxes to put a candle in the middle for a Jack-o'-lantern. It's a wonder we didn't burn something up!"

Also, at another dance which ended with a murder by a character named St Louis. Louis tried preaching to the people at the dance. He was taken outside by some cowboys and asked to leave. He then shot and killed one cowboy. St. Louis served time, then returned to Cleator to live.

Back then, at the get togethers, there certainly wasn't any cussing or swearing in front of the women or the men would take the offender outside to straighten him out.

The school house had special built outhouses for the shit bees, or special imported flies. The inch-long boat shaped flies were ordered in by the Department of Agriculture from the Madagascar jungle. The flies and larva were used to feed on the feces or (Night Fertilizer), thus keeping the outhouses clean. When the town of Cleator had a large population, the outhouses had a large usage. When the mines shut down and the people moved out, the flies died.

To this date, Cleator has 15 original buildings remaining. Founded by James Patrick Cleator, born June 12, 1870 in Dhoon, Machold Parrish, on the Isle of Man in the Irish Sea. With talk of gold in the air, James Cleator, erstwhile sailor turned to prospecting, he found the Bradshaw Mountains to his liking and remained among them the rest of his life. Cleator, Arizona is located at the base of the mighty Bradshaw Mountains, 14 miles west of I-17 exits Bumble Bar open. Photographers welcome, please don't disturb residents. Population: 5 people, 13 dogs.

Chapter Twenty-Five:
How To Be A Good Samaritan
And Got A Busted Foot

By Jim Stewart

1948 Willys Jeep in Crown King

I drove to the Crown King Store to get some fudge. There was a young kid waiting for a vehicle with a Jeep with winch. They were stuck.

We drove to Towers Mountain, to a ravine ¼ mile. There was a Toyota Pickup hanging over a rock ledge, hanging front wheels over and resting on the frame. So, I tied my strap around the tree and began winching out the truck very slowly.

He started it and tried to turn around in a ditch full of pine needles. The back wheels spun out on slick pine needles. I suggested we all get in the back of the truck for weight. The driver of the Toyota gunned it with us in the back. Three of us were thrown into the ditch. I was thrown into the air and came down flat footed in the back of the truck while the truck was bouncing up into the air.

The result was multiple fractures, crutches, walking boot and five months of severe pain. The VA missed the first fractures and took five months to identify with an MRI.

I went up the hill, got on the drive and drove with left foot clutch foot and gas only. There they go right on by past me so I went to Mayer from Crown King, left foot only. The one guy says, "I hope you don't think this was our fault." And they left me knowing I had an injured foot.

If I could have known five months prior, we would have put a pin in your foot, but it's too late now. So, I can give you the cure, 50 mg manganese dosage every day for one year so it is rebuilt all the stretched ligaments and the smashed cartilage between the bones and cured all the foot problems and rebuilt my back problems so I didn't have to have surgery.

Chapter Twenty-Six:
Virgil – Caretaker At The Peck Mine 2013

By Barb Myers

The first time I met Virgil was at the Swastika Mine in 1995. My daughter, Amanda, was two years old. Some friends in Crown King, Ron and Sandy Wells, invited me to go with them to the Peck Mine to see Kelly Painter. It was a beautiful spring day in their old Willy's Jeep. I was so excited to go on this adventure.

When we reached the Swastika Mine, I met John and Mary Ann Hollamon and they had a one-year-old boy named Halem. Also, I met Virgil Snyder. They were all sitting out under a big shade tree. This tree was different, as it would put out droplets of water on you. No one ever did identify the species.

John Hollamon had two Pit Bull dogs that he had to put up. They also had a locked chain

Sam Lowe/ THE PHOENIX GAZETTE

A 100-year-old cabin is home for Kelly Painter, caretaker of an old silver mine in the Bradshaw Mountains.

Caretaker at isolated mine is an (18)90s KIND of GUY

By Sam Lowe
THE PHOENIX GAZETTE

Kelly Painter greeted his visitors with a resounding "halloooool" Then he warned, "Be careful you don't trip over Hormel."

Hormel was standing like a statue in the front yard, scanning the horizon for something else to eat, probably. He's a bit of a fraud but it's not his fault. His original owner thought she was getting a miniature Vietnamese potbellied pig. When the porker far exceeded her size expectations, she hauled him up to Painter's place in the hills. He's definitely potbellied. But miniature he ain't.

Painter doesn't have the foggiest idea how much Hormel weighs and it'll probably always be that way because he doesn't own a scale.

Doesn't own much of anything else practical,

either. It's what you'd expect from someone who has chosen isolation as a way of life.

Painter is 66 and resembles either Gabby Hayes, George Carlin or Glenn Ford with a beard, depending on your age bracket. He moved to the hills a decade ago after one career in the military and another as a hunting outfitter in Alaska. He lives with Hormel and Beulah, a black chicken, deep in the Bradshaw Mountains somewhere between Crown King and the edge of nowhere.

He says he doesn't remember the last time he shaved or had a haircut, but judging from the physical evidence, it's been a while.

Quite a while.

His house is a small cabin perched on a hill and hanging on for dear life. It was built more than

See ■LOWE, Page E4

across the road. Only people that were invited in or people that had the combination could enter. It was not friendly territory to trespassers. They would meet them with a shotgun. We all stopped to visit with John, Mary Ann and Virgil.

We laughed and joked and drank cold beer under the rain-spitting tree. My daughter, Amanda, age two, and Halem, age one, met each other. We left a twelve-pack of beer as a toll charge to get through to go on over the mountain to the Peck Mine.

Ron Wells says, "Hold on!" and up and away over the steep mountain road we went, down into Peck Canyon. We had a great visit with Kelly Painter and his not-so pot belly pig, "Hormel."

Later on, I started taking kids clothes to the Swastika Mine for John and Mary's boy Halem. I would park down the road and walk up to the houses. Later on, I was given the combination to the locked chain. I fell in love with the place. There were two houses and the barn. I later purchased this property in 2002.

100 years ago out of rough-sawn lumber and square nails and was probably used by workmen who toiled in a nearby silver mine. His sisters own it now; he's the caretaker and resident fix-it man, and he answers inquiries into what he does for a living with: "Whatever has to be done."

The remains of old stagecoach routes are the only roads to and from his place. They haven't been repaired since the stages stopped running. It takes a four-wheel-drive and nerves of steel to get in and out, and since that's a damn lot of trouble, he only does it about once a month.

"Like to leave around dawn," he says. "That way, I can beat the traffic jams."

His excursions are not only infrequent; they're also short. He drives into Mayer to pick up his mail and supplies. "If they ain't got it there, I don't need it," he says. Mayer is about 15 miles away as the crow flies. If the crow is driving the same route Painter has to take, it's closer to 30 miles.

His transportation is a large pickup that looks like it's been on the losing side in every battle since the Crusades. "Got it pretty cheap," Painter says. "Used to belong to a little old lady who drove it to church once a week. Had to pay a guy $300 to haul it up here, though."

But it runs. In fact, it purrs. Painter rebuilt the engine himself, removing many of the fancy gadgets found on urban vehicles. And when he fires it up, it hums the sweet melody of an earlier time, a time when he was young and trucks were unencumbered with catalytic devices and monster price tags.

He hauls his own water and built a solar panel arrangement to generate electricity, which he stores in eight car batteries lined up inside the house. They give him enough electrical power to run

Sam Lowe / THE PHOENIX GAZETTE

An old stripped-down Jeep once was Kelly Painter's source of transportation, but it no longer can take the trails.

THE PHOENIX GAZETTE

Painter's cabin is too far out of town to receive TV signals, but a VCR and tapes keep him up to date on movies.

Bradshaws, acquiring a large collection of books and tapes dealing with the area's history. "Not many people know this," he'll say, "but there used to be a big graveyard over there," and he points to some undefined area off to the west.

"But the campers found it. Used the wooden grave markers for firewood. Rotten bastards."

The life is simple, but sometimes

usual. On the other hand, he doesn't have to clean house very often because people don't stop by very often.

Doesn't he ever get lonesome?

"Oh, hell no," he says. "I get sort of horny once in a while, but at my age you don't get lonesome anymore."

He pops open another beer, hoists it in salute to some

One trip to the Swastika, I learned that Virgil had left and was living farther away in a mine tunnel at the Lone Juniper. Since he had no income as he was around age 45 at this time, I started sending up food, blankets, coats, etc. for this man, Virgil. He spent a cold El Nino Winter there.

Virgil Snyder today has been living on the mountain for twenty-five years. He moved up in 1989 while his father, Dewey Snyder, was a caretaker at the mine. Virgil lived at the mine with his father, Dewey, who died from a heart attack. His ashes were scattered over the porch of the long house.

Eventually, John and Mary Ann and boy Halem moved off the mountain and Virgil became the caretaker of the Swastika Mine Group. Amanda and I would go visit on occasion. We would take up some supplies and sometimes we would stay over. I was fascinated by his stories and the view.

In 1999, Lorraine Elliott & Mike Christie, the C.K. Enterprise Company, purchased the Swastika Mine. I arrived one day to find a note on the door, "Gone to Peck Mine", signed Virgil. So over to the Peck I went. He explained that he was no longer living at the Swastika. I helped Virgil move his belongings, a truck load, to the Peck Mine, June 1, 2000.

The Swastika was deserted. I stopped on my way out and threw in a couple bags of sheets, blankets, etc., that we did not have room for on the move over to the Peck Mine. A few days later, I heard the houses had burned down.

Virgil, once by trade, was a machinist for Aero Space in Phoenix. He was also very active at this children's school in the PTO. Since living on the mountain, he has cut trails for rancher John Hunt, so they could ride through. Virgil secured off dangerous mine tunnels and shafts and worked for owner, Virginia Vausner, while living at the Peck.

Today he is working to repair and rebuild the road by hand shovel and pick that was severely washed out from the floods due to the Gladiator Fire in 2012. Virgil has told me he has gotten to see things in nature that others in the city never would see.

I remember him telling me once of a snake that looked like part rattlesnake and part king snake. He had encountered it out on a trail. The snake was mad acting, so Virgil just left it alone. He also has seen an unidentifiable animal that looked part mountain lion and had part hairy fur on it and a long sort of snout nose, some sort of malamute. We called it the Chupacabra, the legendary blood-sucking goat, ugly and dangerous.

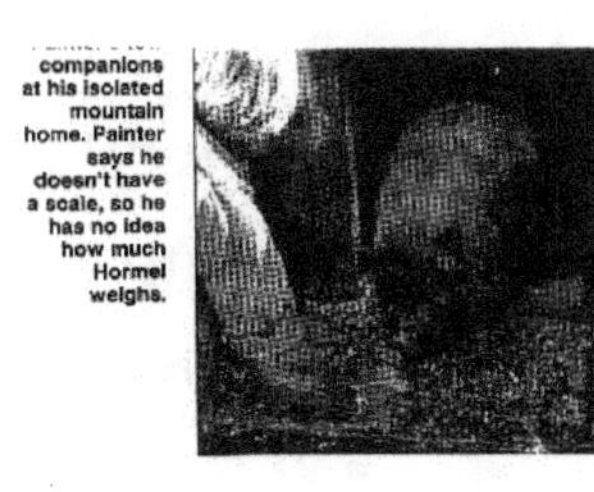

companions at his isolated mountain home. Painter says he doesn't have a scale, so he has no idea how much Hormel weighs.

By Sam Lowe
THE PHOENIX GAZETTE

Kelly Painter greeted his visitors with a resounding "hallooooo!" Then he warned, "Be careful you don't trip over Hormel."

Hormel was standing like a statue in the front yard, scanning the horizon for something else to eat, probably. He's a bit of a fraud but it's not his fault. His original owner thought she was getting a miniature Vietnamese potbellied pig. When the porker far exceeded her size expectations, she hauled him up to Painter's place in the hills. He's definitely potbellied. But miniature he ain't.

Painter doesn't have the foggiest idea how much Hormel weighs and it'll probably always be that way because he doesn't own a scale.

either. It's what you'd expect from someone who has chosen isolation as a way of life.

Painter is 66 and resembles either Gabby Hayes, George Carlin or Glenn Ford with a beard, depending on your age bracket. He moved to the hills a decade ago after one career in the military and another as a hunting outfitter in Alaska. He lives with Hormel and Beulah, a black chicken, deep in the Bradshaw Mountains somewhere between Crown King and the edge of nowhere.

He says he doesn't remember the last time he shaved or had a haircut, but judging from the physical evidence, it's been a while.

Quite a while.

His house is a small cabin perched on a hill and hanging on for dear life. It was built more than

Another time John Hollamon was visiting Virgil at the Peck. John is a big tall man and he does not scare. Well, this night it was pitch dark out. John was outside going to the bathroom. He ran back inside the cabin shaking. He said something ran up to him that was on two legs. It was very tall and hairy. The creature looked him in the eye and then turned and ran off. Later on, when I went there and heard the story, we set traps up and alarms, beer cans on a wire as to alert us of any intruders. We heard nothing, but we were very cautious when going outside.

On another occasion, while Virgil was cutting trail for the ranchers, he had a camp set up in Peck Canyon. The bears were in full force tearing up the camp, messing with the gas cans and chain saws. One day Virgil was out working on a trail. A bear appeared and came towards him. Virgil says, "I didn't know what to do. I didn't think I could outrun the bear, so I talked to it."

The bear stood there for a little while, then turned away and left. Virgil and the bear looked into each other's eyes while Virgil talked to the bear. The bear wanted to follow him home.

Virgil's birds in Peck Canyon are incredible. They expect food from him daily. He can call them to come in and he talks to the black ravens. The blue birds are very good watch birds. They will signal an alert if there is a rattlesnake or any predator, owls, foxes, skunks, hawks, in the canyon. The blue birds will squawk and flutter around the area where a predator is.

Also, Virgil has a sort of tame bobcat. His name is Long Legs. Long Legs has been living near the cabin since he was very young. The bobcat would come and try to catch one of the birds. But he sat out in the open where all could see him. Finally, the bobcat did learn to hid and pounce to get his meal. Virgil would sometimes encounter the bobcat around the cabin area. He would get up near three foot close to him. He was kind of friendly, but still wild. "They had a respect for each other's space." Virgil says.

One day I went to see Virgil. It looked like flour had been spilled all over the porch area. He came out and says, "There was a big bull snake that went up into the attic." He was waiting for it to come back out, so he could close up that opening. The flour was sprinkled out so he could see the snake's tracks of departure. But so far, the snake has not come out.

Virgil is a true humanitarian or nature lover, per se. He is the only person I have ever seen to stop, get out of the car and turn over a beetle bug that was upside down, to save its life.

Chapter Twenty-Seven:
Dusty Pages Of Arizona Past
And Present 2009

By Laurence L. Fleshner

Alexandra's

Explore, high, in the Bradshaw Mountains
And find the Peck Mine, which was
Found by four.

They found it difficult to transport ore.
So, a Tea Stamp Mill was erected
Near the mines with the ore.

Between seventy-five and
One hundred buildings
Was hard to ignore.

Telling people
How to get to a town
Without a name,
Became quite a chore.

Then one day Mrs. T. M. Alexander
Became the first lady
To visit the Mine décor.

So impressed was the town
To the core,
Alexandra's name became
This town's lore.

However, Alexandra had a
Major problem that soon
Became an open sore.

Litigation by the four,
Resulted in the mine money
Going to lawyers
In Prescott with a pour.

With no profits and an
On-coming war.
Alexander the town
Was no more.

But today nothing will be found
Of this mining town
Not so much as a door.

Above this town
Was the old Swastika Mine,
That many have come
To explore.

Renamed the
Silver Prince Mine
Barb will not sell you
Her small store.

Famous Outhouses

In the Bradshaw Mtns.

Grey House Outhouse

New Flush Toilets Old Salon 1995

High Class Outhouse

Dallas Casey - Star Island

Cleator School House Outhouse

Cleator School House - Girls

Cleator School House - Boys

Crown King Outhouse

AY Ranch Cleator Outhouse

Old Cordes Outhouses

Song

By Barb Myers

End of the Trail

Come on everybody.
Let's make like a cow patty and hit the trail.
Come on everybody,
"Mount up" and hit that trail.
Come on, let me show you,
The end of the trail.
Here's to the cowboys,
It's all happening at the end of the trail.
'Tis been a long hard trail,
It's gotta get opened up,
The grass is green.
Gotta gets those cows up on that trail.
Here's to the cowboys.
Here's to the cowboys.
It's all on the mountain,
At the end of the trail.
Come on everybody,
Let's go see what's happening
At the end of the trail.

"End of the Trail Party"

Friday, March 13th to

Friday, March 20th.

Never happened.

I wrote this song.

Readings and References:

Bruce M. Wilson, "Crown King and the Southern Bradshaws: A Complete History," (Chandler, AZ: Crown King Press, 1990).

John R. Signor, "The Crown King District," The Warbonnet, Santa FE Railway Historical and Modeling Society, 18, no. 3 (2011) 13-32.

Cleator's New Rock School House: circa 1931- Special from CNN

www.ingramcontent.com/pod-product-compliance
Lightning Source LLC
Chambersburg PA
CBHW051653060726
47593CB00021B/715